GREAT SILENT BALLAD

ALSO BY A. F. MORITZ

Poetry

Here
Black Orchid
Between the Root and the Flower
The Visitation
The Tradition
Song of Fear
The Ruined Cottage
Ciudad interior
Phantoms in the Ark
Mahoning
Houseboat on the Styx
Rest on the Flight into Egypt
The End of the Age
Conflicting Desire
Early Poems
Night Street Repairs
The Sentinel
The New Measures
Sequence
The Sparrow: Selected Poems
As Far As You Know
The Garden

As Editor

The Best Canadian Poetry in English, 2009
The 2010 Griffin Poetry Prize Anthology
The 2024 Griffin Poetry Prize Anthology

Translation

Children of the Quadrilateral: Selected Poetry of Benjamin Péret
Testament for Man: Selected Poems of Gilberto Meza

Translation of Works by Ludwig Zeller

Ludwig Zeller in the Country of the Antipodes: Poems 1964–1979
The Marble Head and Other Poems
The Ghost's Tattoos
Body of Insomnia and Other Poems
Rio Loa: Station of Dreams
Woman in Dream
The Rules of the Game: Selected Shorter Poems 1952–2008
For a Savage Love: Three Books

GREAT SILENT BALLAD

POEMS

A. F. Moritz

Published in Canada in 2024 and the USA in 2024 by House of Anansi Press Inc.
houseofanansi.com

House of Anansi Press is a Global Certified Accessible™ (GCA by Benetech) publisher. The ebook version of this book meets stringent accessibility standards and is available to readers with print disabilities.

28 27 26 25 24   1 2 3 4 5

Library and Archives Canada Cataloguing in Publication
Title: Great silent ballad : poems / A.F. Moritz.
Names: Moritz, A. F. (Albert Frank), author.
Identifiers: Canadiana (print) 20240330676 | Canadiana (ebook) 20240330684 | ISBN 9781487012960 (softcover) | ISBN 9781487012977 (EPUB)
Subjects: LCGFT: Poetry.
Classification: LCC PS8576.O724 G74 2024 | DDC C811/.54—dc23

Cover design: Greg Tabor
Cover image: *The Virgin and Child Enthroned* by Cosimo Tura

House of Anansi Press is grateful for the privilege to work on and create from the Traditional Territory of many Nations, including the Anishinabeg, the Wendat, and the Haudenosaunee, as well as the Treaty Lands of the Mississaugas of the Credit.

With the participation of the Government of Canada
Avec la participation du gouvernement du Canada | Canada

We acknowledge for their financial support of our publishing program the Canada Council for the Arts, the Ontario Arts Council, and the Government of Canada.

Printed and bound in Canada

CONTENTS

The Tawer

As I write out my poems
will I come to the one perfect to head my book?
Or will it still have to be written?
And so, intention will ruin it.

As I write out my poems
I see how poor were the songs I sung
with so much pleasure, so much oblivion
to lonesomeness and stillness.
How dishevelled they were, with none
of the beauty of petal-scrap tatterdemalions
carried away by a wind devil.

As I write out my poems
they are revised before my eyes.
It's wonderful to see them again as they half change
into arguments, these birds, stars, and trees
that formerly were girls and phalluses, these plashes
and gleams that once came from imprisonment, that have been blood
let by an edge of polished jade.

Sifting these notes of mine, longing
for a beginning that is not a longing
to begin, a dawn to be dawn not dawn's herald,
I search for the song that has already been.
As I write out my poems.

GREAT SILENT BALLAD

Beyond

During that sweet time when there is no death
there's always someone dying, somewhere, outside.
And maybe not. I can't be everywhere. I don't know.
Simply the mind's eye goes to what is known
from getting accustomed to the earth: anguish.
The mind's eye produces images on its own,
a rigid plot and characters of fate, a beautiful
setting with smoking spots and heaps of damage.
And it could be that this novel
is the fallen angel of late...I mean, of light,
the examiner, the tempter, the idiot questioner
who asks and asks and never answers on the plea
nobody can. And I myself am that Satan. Happiness
was shrieking all around me in there like an imp of flame
with two dozen heads. I slipped outside. Should I try
to sober up? I was closer here, in the alley, to the wars
and hospitals. My elegant shoes in the mud,
trash, and drops of ill-aimed piss. Should I walk away,
maybe past paramedics loading a gurney
where they've thrown an institutional cloth across
some shrieks or a perfect stillness? The beloved
progression, the four chords, with its blue rhythms,
heartbeat of our people, leaks through the wall
of concrete block. Yes, truly, I tell you, it's an ill
wind that blows no good. There's still the time
to celebrate. We are not yet one of those
who lie beyond us. Let's go back in.

Folk Blues

The singer knows
what it is to be dead.
He's been found and lost
found and lost repeatedly
in his paltry eight decades
and now will he be found
once more so late? In the times lost
it truly was to be dead
in hollow lands to wander
among the shades
though he had a wife there
and an old car
and there was a booze can
fronting the river
he liked to frequent
where the wind came in
through the slate and in summer
he sat on the rickety
narrow verandah
shaded from noon
with two old friends
older than he was
who never had a record
and pretended not to care
that once he did.
They all together
beat on their guitars
each in turn to admire
the tricks of their fingers
talked a little took a drink
went silent stared across

the shimmering water to think
and thought nothing
for a long time
there on the Natchez side.
Would the river still
pass down along
would it keep on passing?
And that's how it was
the times he died.

Dancer Speaking

What is the dance? A naked girl,
invisible, and I am naked dancing
so you can see it. Tomorrow
you'll see the dance in some other
body. I wish I could pass away
as I ceased my portrayal of it,
and not be a rind waiting
as the next comes on.

And the naked girl is a woman too,
and she and a man are the dance
in the boîte de nuit
as the brass choir stands for its chorus
and lifts up the shining, skirling bells
of the horns. "I fall in love
too easily." It's all invisible. So we
ceremoniously put on evening dress
and come here, twirl

and make that there be
the club and orchestra for a world tonight. Our world
and we in its midst so the dance
may be seen. I wish we could pass away
into the moonlight beyond the doors
open to a deserted garden,
but we go back
to the browning rind,
home, arguing, our doors slamming,

our crying. Until one leaves and one
remains. Both singing so that the great silent

ballad can be heard. Love and regret
and love again, love returning at a safe
distance—the memory, a dream,
of the lost one
who was intolerable in the body
and is beautiful, everything,
in yearning.

A Muse

The sullen stiffness of the flute, metal on which
the flicked fingernail clicks...the stiff
vainglory glinting blind silver in the sun...
played, it sends out a stream that is nothing but water's
invisible sinuosity—stream without banks, without
a beautiful land to sparkle in. Flowing everywhere,
where it wants, where it has to, bringing shores
and woods to mind, places where travellers
would stop beside it, stories, bends of a river
to be the sites of cities—cities of hope,
hope that then and there the cities to be built
will be better...even good.

The sullen stiffness
of the foot, which seems a claw enveloped
in stretched humanish stuff, like a poor woman's
foxed gauze that she hoarded up against a coming
clothless future, and it lies there now wrapping
some treasure of old, bent knives...the foot that seems to be
trying to talon-pierce the ground in bitter resolve
to be a root, a rock...the rot-purple foot
opens inside. A little door there, in that dark room
in that gnarled hovel, leads to the inner fires.
A tunnel descends, a stair ascends from a hidden alcove
to the smaller and the greater fires, the one above
and the one below, heart and core,
blood-warmth and magma.

O Terpsichore!
Such is the playing of the instrument.
Such is the dance in its first step before

a step is taken, when you, goddess vowel
of the beginning, begin to word the lyric.

I Was a Useless Man

I was a useless man, and being unused,
I was elderly at twenty-eight. Then one day
God came to me in the form of a young girl.
God only knows why she had inspired hate,
but she had to flee and escape, and had to get to
only she knew where. So she led. I followed,
but had to go first—there were certain things we'd meet
that I had to meet, things I could do that I had to.
Push aside heavy broken concrete blocks.
Turn big rusting screws in half-threaded holes
in thick metal plates. Put an axe through the heads
of men who came against us, though they were men
like me, I suppose: I don't know why they came
and tried to kill her and why they should be dead
and if they had invented killing her for themselves
or were moved only by an ersatz frenzy of
having been employed by someone for the purpose.
After my struggles, she'd come abreast and lay me on a bed
of tires and rags, and cry, suturing my wounds,
and we'd rest and go on. It was in the poor east end
of the city, always dark, with bricks and twists
of aluminum, crushed bicycles, cars without wheels,
all around. No open store. The spit on the sidewalks
had dried out years ago. The discarded cans
were razors. She had to make it through that
to the dawn gate. After three days we reached it.
It was vast and locked and filthy. I gave her
my last aid, smashing through the rotted wood.
Then ducking through the shape I'd made,
she was gone. Outside. I turned to go back.
But why? I stayed there near the wall. That once,

three days, I had had something to do.
I've sometimes remembered and repeated it all,
all my life. I am now one hundred and twenty-eight.

The Little Known

The little known
lover in anguish
and peace rules nothing,
wants not anything
to be ruled—true daughter
of true god—everything just
come to her, divine
gift, her example. In a city
a wide wilderness of towers
she elects a low one
and ascends to a middle storey
to live there awhile
and look across
her realm. The walls
close in around their goddess
like glass leafage to fold her
in hard capes—all
they can do. To one another
in vacant and solemn grief
they shine their faces onto captured
crystal tablets, square
and empty—their images
hover on each other's
blank bodies, they are
each other's faces!
She looks out at them,
they reflect like worlds
in drops of dew
on green leaves. To her
audience then arrives
the air ambulance

beating, lifting from
the heliport on the hospital roof
to carry help to some
maiming, some entrapment
in twisted metal, some
desperation on the highway. The land too
pays tribute. Trucks flow
in ponderous spate
down the long pavement
with cartons of oranges,
beef sides, pecans, tomatoes,
frozen turkeys, curiously
concocted draughts
of every colour...hopeless
to name or picture it—all
foods that there are
huddling to her dawn
levee from immense
gathering places—depots near
the city gates. But her city
has no gates. It disperses
gently past fraying houses
to prosperous farmsteads, then
over rivers, moraines,
escarpments, while she takes in
her vast sunset through the cracks
between high built barriers, through the song
of cranes and drills. Geese also
fly over, sometimes a pair
negotiating low along
strict paths among glass cliffs
at tenth-storey level. Blown
snow, rain, and low sunlight
lighting empty walls, shining

upward from beneath
gold and purple cloud bars, serve
her famous demesne. Standing
in her high cube, she breathes
the humid evening cooling
over harvest-heavy
wheat fields of memory's
imagining—young days, long
gone evenings where lightning bugs
blaze in the tassels. Only her body
equals the scent of rich
laden freshness this
month in the far fields that serve
her city. August. Her birthday
is coming soon.

A Woman in a Painting but Not So

She struggles with her lumpy bulk,
something in a whitish rope-shut sack
of grey cloth—vegetables? clothing?—
and her thick-heeled shoes don't help her
nor her heavy skirt, slate blue, that shows
the hems of heavy underskirts, bemudded.
She drags—burden, costume, body through a mist
sand-fine, pinpointed in November wind
that pushes back along the way she comes,
strong but not strong enough
to stop her or even bend the dry
branches. Just strong enough to make
the river choppy, flowing at her right hand,
water like clay, as she reaches
the village houses. The painter
never saw her. Corot was not there
that torpid dawn—when was it, 1750...
1350? Only the squelch of her footfalls,
slap of small waves, wind ruffling. Still,
Corot was with her and took her up
whenever, later, elsewhere, he took up the fields,
the rivers, paths, and people. She was there
before him and he also painted her things
that can't be seen. Her rote prayers
to the Virgin that had redoubled her pity,
had been her wisdom. And something else,
unheard but part of the quiet
of the vision of her
in which she does not appear: the trudge
of desire. There
is desire past eagerness, past expectation,

joy in her heart who can't feel it
in the present and expected pain.

Credal Statement

I'm not a modern man. I never believed
that all is torture, loss, frustration because words
fail to attain what we love, fail to save it,
to carry as in a beautiful rush basket
woven by the girls of our tribe all the incomparable
beauties, a dandelion by a fence post,
a night with stars as big as honeydews
whirling in the sky once over southern France.
Over Great Zimbabwe. Over humid Ohio
four hundred million years ago when it waited
on the yet unshifted rock three hundred miles
below the equator. Words are beings, are
for being, not to be
adequate to things. Things are not adequate to things.
That groundhog I love isn't adequate
to this grasshopper, to that slow creek, to the sky
in its configuration above this spot
years ago in a crystal January night
as I walked up to the doors to enter and hear
Maynard Ferguson. Things are not adequate to words.
A phrase is a body among bodies.
One of your bodies. This gives life, gives life
even to your doubting the adequacy of words:
you said it so it's a pit
you truly did fall into, you
and your sentence. That is a living history.
That is a tragic drama of a world.

To Those Who Like to Say "I'm Not Much for Poetry"

I don't mind that you scorn or ignore my beloved vocation.
You don't live without poetry.
That statement, in the way of poetry
that you scorn or ignore, means several things.
You don't live if there's no poetry: you don't live
at all, or if you appear to yourself to be living, you're not.
You really are living, though, even if you're dead,
because you do have poetry, poetry's with you
whether you know it or not, whether you think so or don't.
Poetry's there in the earth and waters and light and wind,
a shelf too high for you, bawling child, even to see what's on it,
but there are always people who, for some reason,
love you so much
that they hand it down for free.

Dead Skunk in the Road

They were gathered around a smashed skunk
on the street in front of my porch. I counted
about seven billion, not precisely,
but close enough. After all, what do they think
they matter in detail? They were all deciding
that the skunk was what they are.
It would fester there on the asphalt
and some tread prints of its blood
in the middle of their circle. The one thing
visible to everybody. It would stink awhile
before achieving mummification by the sun.
They'd leave it there. Apparently they still thought
they required an icon of meaning.
But later someone would scrape it up.

It was clear, looking at them from the porch,
what was the nature of the object,
the outside world.

For one who thinks of great destiny,
destined but endlessly opening, there is
great destiny. For one who thinks
that the carelessly murdered skunk,
sleek lovely friend and pest of our backyard
that summer, is dead, there's nothing.
Not the skunk, street, lawnmower, adventure
vacation to Nepal with empty splendour far below
the mountain passes, the deoxyribose,
the Riemann tensor. Not the idea.
For anyone who waits, thinking of our friend
of that summer, the skunk,

there is marvellous destiny.
As long as there are two who think this way
in the city, the rest are safe in nothingness,
for what those two think is not
just what they think.

What Now

When I was dead, two females came
and sat down on the couch, one at my foot, one at my head.
Where am I? Let's see. I was beyond aware
of them and all about them, of how they sit
erect so easily, a poise before comportment,
a care above self-abnegation in devotion,
a dedication ignorant of "instead,"
instead attending to desire—a greedy angelic
deportment in the human. Play and rest. Leisure.
Love of another, ultimate pleasure, limit of
self-seeking. I was beyond being aware whether
I loved more their love for me or the love
that each held for her sister. Their intimate
stillness must have shored me from the waste of knowledge.

I was in the green island of perception, asleep.
Its green as always drew shadow over its rocks
in the fire from particles or stars. Perception:
green island in the salt, wadi in ruined sand...
in the freeze of furious satellites, pilgrim world—
blue runnels, flowers of all colours, air that stands,
sighs, or rages, fresh as an infant, a razor. The waste
spread out beneath it imperceptible—the known,
what the animal can't know. I was in the little
that eyes of jaguarundi, kinglet, squid, the ant's feelers,
all nostrils, tongues, and cilia redeem
from the untouchable. There, I being dead,
two females came and sat down on the couch
to listen for me, one at my foot, one at my head.

A Flower Giving Names to Eve and Adam

Here is this striking flower, love—what shall we
call it? We came out here
and tramped these unbound meadows, in and out
of copses of larch and elder, and met things
we knew of—coreopsis, the golden prairie tickseed: one example—
and many we didn't. We came out here
without a dictionary. If we want to call this thing
or recall it between us now, as long as we're here,
we'll have to make it a name of our own,
like the ones we've made each other—
there are so many! One for every freak
of every season and hour of your heart's weather
and mine, so many designations of each ripple
and gust in our inner wafts and storms,
tender nicknames for every bodily tic
of eyelid or lip. You have so many names
between us, you've given me so many! Will we give
this striking flower just one? Maybe for now, so we
can talk about it now, while we're alone here.
Maybe when we go back we can look up
what they all agreed to call it, and then it will seem just
to have a certain word. But never
in our hearts. We'll go farther—search
and research!—and we'll learn the list
of the flower's ancient labels in a thousand small
lost tongues—what grandmothers
and grandmothers of grandmothers called it
in many countries. But we'll know
its secret name, the one it took for then
when we were with it in ignorance—our name for it,
its name for us. We know and the flower knows

how it’s a fountain of names, all one,
for everyone who comes.

Where

These visions. Some might say I saw them
because I read poetry and became
disposed to astonishment. Some might say
because I was disposed to astonishment
I read poetry. The two parties might debate
cause and effect, chicken and egg. In fact,
no one will say anything. This poem will rest
undisturbed, one of the few things in the world
left respectfully not-dug-up. Like woods
in central Maine, virgin because too remote
to be exploited. Like a stream in Ohio
where industry collapsed, so the water went
fresh again. Like a boy whose parents don't care
where he gets to. The useless is there and continues.
On economically unviable steeps of rock,
under far evergreens, the mountain potentilla
that once I saw still grows. In my looking at it
many years ago...that's where I am buried.

WHY DO WE READ?

Why Do We Read?

Why do we read? For pleasure? And back when reading
could only be listening,
was that for pleasure—to have
                                        to love

to hear the invisible
perimeters of the family enclave intoned
while we squat, walled in the visible,

the shadow scatter of huts of skin, the limit
of the firelight, rustling of leaves,
chirring of beasts?
                              Was Shelley

constructing pleasure while being harried
across Europe by despair and scorn, by need,
his own rash generosity

giving away what he had to
live on? Do we suppose
he sat there sometimes writing, exempli gratia:

“Many a green isle needs must be
In the deep wide sea of misery,”
so that someone sitting in a garden

might thrill with awe, then turn
to wonder: Why so many ee’s? too many?
And the metre—is it too swingy?

And so for a while the knowledge of his art,
and the critique, holds me
above the subject. And this is pleasure

until again the poem overcomes, absorbs me,
my guard or my distraction softly
annihilated, my pointless intellection, and I find myself again

with beauty and anguish
on the downward slope to death. I've been
thrown out of the paradise of being,

my being. In that paradise, neither the poem nor the morning
moves, nothing is moving as the breeze
trembles the leaves, the sun passes over, gentle shadows

shift to the west, and time is eternal, my toy,
and being my toy, is real for once. I've been
thrown out of the paradise of living

into the hell of becoming, which goes badly
always, despite what the would-be happy
prophets of energy, our great

grandparents, used to say, moved
to tears and frenzy by the brutal surprise
of their old discovery—everything is motion.

Or have I been given back to reality? Released
from childhood's mythological sensuous dream
by a benevolent myth, the poem, come to lead me

out of the hells of falsehood of its own Arcady
into the sudden opening of the eyes,

in which I die.
                                        Now my childhood lies

in inexplicable ruin, in insular
fragments, enigmatic, too few remaining
of what was broken, whatever it was, to piece

into a text. But I love above everything else
to read those smoking stones, those cold bricks
with glyphic char marks. Home sickness. Home, because

who knew the figure of that world
was passing away, like this one? so permanently
we lived in it.
                                        No, Enheduanna was probably

intending pleasure only secondarily when she led
the chorus into the temple of She who later became
Astarte and Aphrodite-Diana and then died.

Died in fact long before Herostratus
burned down her house. Died into merely the moon,
on which we are now setting up tents—like Baudelaire

camping under the breasts of his giantess, a move
repeated not long ago by Almodóvar,
and by me a little earlier. No, the chief priestess

was probably intending dominance
for her father Sargon by devouring into his goddess
all the goddesses of the conquered. The hearers

heard mainly this. They hardly noticed
how the tears of things—oh more powerfully, stabbingly

after the revolution of Lugal-Ane, in the hymn,

Nin me šara, of the priestess alone, without a temple,
wandering...the tears erupt through the words, wonderful,
like smoke from incense or from burning meat:

horror, pride, and baffled unknowing at her own body
and its functioning given over to fate,
as the actions of conquerors are. That she must live.

That disaster impregnates. With imprecations, desires,
memories, songs—to yourself, to the goddess, the dead?
How not to find in her (as Montale said of the poor eel

seeking a home in drying ponds—in the tiny repetitious
lakes of a watery landscape seen in dreams
by Juan Ramón)...how not find in her a sister: great voice

thrown out to the wilds, where lions roam.
The only freedom: to know that you are driven, or deny it,
or to lie down and be a pebble by the road:

✲

You are the form-making place.
You spread fear,
O Lady of the Mountain, place of fear.
Your deep womb is dark,
Your flesh towers above us all
Pouring shadow over the wildernesses and the high plateaus.
Ancient incantations fixed you in place.
In you the light is always murky and low.
Even the moon can't enter there.
Only the Goddess of Birth gives beauty to your caves.
The princess
Princess of silence
Never-failing Queen of Heaven
(Heaven quakes when she speaks)
Has built you, fastened you there, made you be
A house, a mountain,
A womb, a rough-shelled possession of darkness
Shining on us
In this shining place.

*

O pebble pebble by the road,
you alone know
the secret of humility

Does the garden of eternity
lurk in the dusty
inch of your face

In you
    in what appears
darkness and silence
is there the favored space

where the endless greenwood
and the talk of lovers inhere—
the space that is everyplace

Pebble pebble
        all that I would
truly like to know
          here
at the opposite end of history

from Sargon the Great
is how to go home happily
along the road knowing good

*

And so it ended,
my lecture scarcely begun,
suddenly interrupted by two songs,
who were the only audience
that had been curious enough to come,
and who went away together laughing
as soon as they had sung.

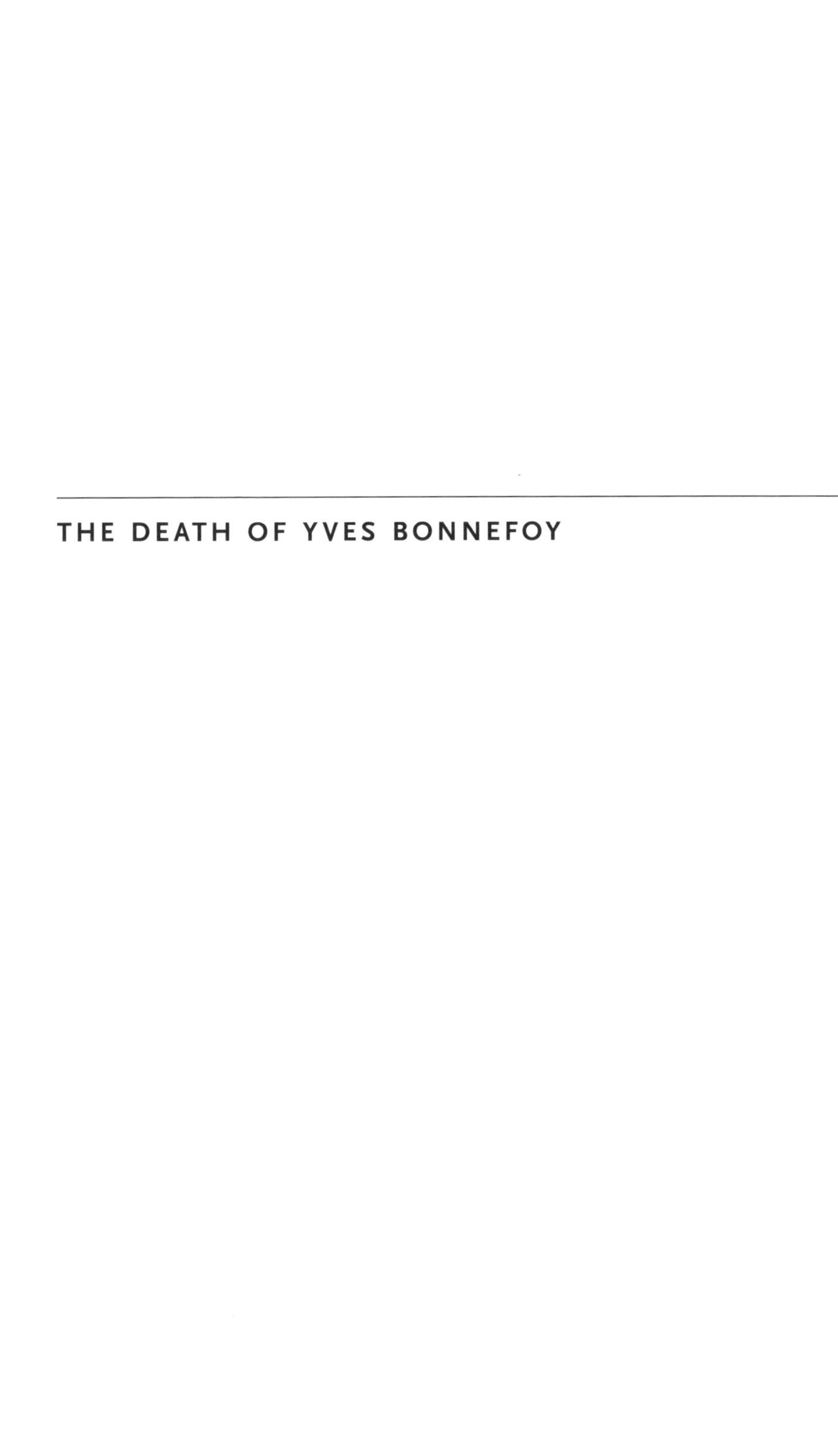

THE DEATH OF YVES BONNEFOY

The Death of Yves Bonnefoy

So a world is gone
and it calls us—how can this be,
a world with a voice? It must be another
kind of world, when ours
is the one world and that other
was always only this one and now has passed
not away but into here. The world has no voice,
its ambassador does. And here he is
invisible. A singing
as talk it seems at times should be. It's like
a composer, divine, crafty and unrelenting,
beginning to write (and the audience
already hearing) in an upper room,
in a tenement second storey not far above
the garbage stacked in black plastic bags along the curb,
not far from sharp then muffled shouts—
violence, despair—and a distant sobbing,
the soughing of wind in apple trees
around an old farmhouse looking out on the hills
so that when the musician lifts his eyes, it's the sun,
mounded clouds, sheep on the slopes,
and when he gazes below it's martins
playing in the leaves and a glimpse through that
labyrinth of theirs
down to shining grass
and nasturtium beds that those birds see beneath them
by a sandstone wall...
so it goes in his music. And this is

the way he's written us. Our every flat greeting,
swear word, explanation, lie,

what we mean or once meant perfectly
set to the orchestra of our voice
when it was real. If ever. As in him it is real
inside its own cursing, its sliding away...
And we're an opera of the ordinary days,
a folk song, ruined epochs
and adequate seconds in their beauty
now as they're written. Now. Not
in nostalgia. Not after death
and vanishing have purged the failure
and the living one's memory of the miserable
dead is clean
and there can be pure grief at last and a smile
comes out after long overcast.

Can it be that a voice like that
falls into the old quest passed, nostalgia,
the same way a singing cricket of late August slips
toward winter's venture, slips
into the cut, the crevice, silence? But it exists.
The voice, the beloved, the cricket alive
in the once and future. In the once and future,
you are the "and"—and here
and now you join and read the once
and future crickets' bones
in the voice, with the voice. This guide
gives much interest and hope
to this landscape and its city
that had threatened to be a museum
despite incessantly replacing itself with more
angles, materials, metallic lights, synthetic
noises and smells, more invisible
operative cubes. More of you. Of me. The voice
came inside my ear, became my ear, and I saw

it was silence—had been silence
already when it lived and spoke out loud
with its humid tongue. And action,
no stronger than a flower,
belongs to it. It points back,
always back to the flower from
its word, the same old word—flower—that it makes
the prime act now. From the beginning
it was a flower. It is a flower!

Flower, word, and death—let there be death.
He would not overcome time: he was time:
the flower with its roots and wet soil,
with its air and sun. From where the weak stem fountains
up from the ground we set
out again. Through the mechanics
endlessly ahead, the path is
back through this other world.

Vagueness

Pushing and hacking through the haze
of close branches, we stumbled on a bank or shore
at a small cove: a sort of tunnel of leaves
screening us off above and left and right,
the far end of its floor giving on the water.
The water was trembling at our feet, grey
and wild-grape-dusty blue and faint mauve
and some colour like sunburnt old clay. Fog wrapped it,
steaming from its surface and floating from the sky,
just gauzy enough to reveal how immensely far
the other side must be, heavy enough to obscure
whether the body of water was long or round,
whether the quivering wavelets were a current, a lake's
nervous containment, or the edge of an ocean lapping.
We couldn't see if the sudden brief bubbling sounds
were fish leaping, muskrats or lizards gliding,
something unknown, illusions of our ears.
Everything there was thick and certain, pressing in
on our eyes, skin, and throats. Everything
was vague. All we could see was at last
we'd reached the serious place.

An Angel

That you stand here admiring
everything
is the meaning of what is termed "hard to believe."

It's hard to believe in engaging the interest of a being
whose feet are beside me while its eyes engulf
a Lyman-break galaxy, and the manufacture of stars
occurs inside them while here they look
at this water-strider as I do and also from within its thorax
and from all other vantages and angles, mostly
unknowable—too strange for us even to desire.

You extend through the known and the unsuspected. You travel
by simple being-throughout. Yet we've imagined you
envying our bodies. Here supposedly you look
at our arguments in bed, bad handwriting,
decaying food, a toy lamb missing its head,
elegant plates we throw away in favor of better ones,
throw away in the face of the poor, who can't hope
to buy such things—you watch them glancing every way
to avoid the guardians posted on the garbage, then scurrying off
with their takings...you look at all that
with affection. Affection? A blank-like gaze
without a name. So we throw words at it
like wonder. Like admiration.

We imagine that, immense in the immense,
you can see us without belittlement.
That you've been sent to serve us. Here,
prince, there has never been any royalty but you—
invisible, but appearing now and then, we say,

for instance in a bird's wing, an easy
lilt of glide
joining here to there.

Mentioning

What does it matter if that poet's philosophy was correct
or erroneous? It led him to mention many things.
In all the works of the most achieved philosopher,
who had arrived at the vision of plenitude
and then at plenitude itself
through a terrible combat with nothingness,
there is nothing. Not an animal, plant, anklet, amulet, snowflake.
Not a scent, an old ballad, a sudden motion
at the corner of the eye. Scarcely even "animal,"
scarcely "jewellery." There is nothing,
only plenitude. The poet aspired erroneously
to convert himself into soul, climbing the antique stairs of love
or contemplation to *l'esprit pur,* and on the way
he passed, and like some dog could not help turning aside to,
a teddy bear, a watchtower, the mother shattered in the bombing,
the innocent stumblers being herded toward a train or
disappearing
into factory hangar doors or timber-propped mine mouths,
the fox kit in its fur, a smashed ant, its front half still struggling,
this willow tree, this one, standing and whispering right here,
that the big people cut down despite all cries
in that poet's fifth year...I could go on but if I did
you wouldn't believe me, because all this
goes on and on, is proof of eternity, the innumerable,
where each item, each moment of an item, is
a greater world than the world. This was his mentioning. In it,
all of this passed—hidden under a wet oak leaf
on a forest floor where no one will ever come, or in an alley
at night with used syringes in the paste of grime and oil
where someone sometimes sees. His mentioning
was a turning aside and stopping, a being stopped,

a love at first sight, a falling in love. Such was his never finished
and essentially nonexistent quest, the result of his delusions
in the nonsense of gnosticism and alchemy. The gift
of the Fata Morgana of pure spirit: the lumber room of a life
where touring through the assorted scraps
you saw all things that ever
had been cut down and sawn into parts
whispering: green branches. So you see
the cobweb-shadowed piles of lumber: dew on leaves
lit with upward rays at dawn, freshness
arranged in unforeseen orders of pleasure and shock.

A Meditation

I sat down to still myself, arrive at no mind,
and await the coming of the voice of the spirit
or the presence of nothing. As usual, my breath,
on which I should embark my soul to be carried
by the slowly quieting spate into the depths of my lungs
and of being, drove me half crazy. An ever more narrowed,
more trapped, desperate awareness
of everything—musky on a hook—that turned to blood
in the throat, turned to kaleidoscope, turned to touching
the fire-sound and every fragment of a bomb
in the instant of blast. Turned to a being devoured
in a blastula of vegetating dawn.

Then there came a poem. Then there was nothing left
but a spring
in my heart and legs. I leapt at the command
and ran and wrote the lines, sweating, as usual,
sweat dropping in gobbets from my armpits—
a summer rain once the lightning passes
with the winds, then the light pattering too
ends, and a scent of ozone comes
penetrating from the high stillness and twilight
over far-off wooded ridges. This
was what was in the lines, and the spirit,
or nothingness,
unless this was it, I forgot.

Word and Silence: After Neruda

The word was born in the blood
and grew up in the dark body,
pulsing. It came from lands of stone
and lands of wedded soil and water: mud, marl.
Farmers raised it: bitter outdoor work, the word,
work with the dead and the unborn. It came out
from the darkness that it contains:
affirmation, clarity and power,
destruction, negation, death.
I drink, and all that I have to drink is,
the word that I say: endless water, my mother,
fountain of song, origin of the mouth
producing it, giver of the commandments
silent in its future. Giver of the life
it rose from. I say it and I am
and that way alone I move near,
nearer and nearer, to its silence.

My hands in this emptiness gather
bunches of grapes,
night that cannot be weighed,
the families of the stars, a choir
more silent than silence,
a sound from the moon—
oceanic night, a wavering,
about to open,
of soft cloths and wings—
a deep arrival
overflowing its names.

Here between the light and the water, silent

symbol, is the tower
from which I watch time with its sword
and then press forward to live.
I inhale all of the air. The desert
building up in the city
to cover it
drives me mad
and I talk to myself without knowing who that is
picking petals there
from the silence on high.

The Gift

I've long given up the dream
of having something to do
with the coming of the good kingdom.
Just let it be coming and let me live
over to one side
and then when it arrives let me live
in one of its rooms off one of its alleys.
It will be plenty simply finally
not to fear my own filth, the puzzle
of the whereabouts of food, the rain
of muddy plaster spheres always falling
a little late, mirroring beneath my ceiling
the pure rain after it starts hitting
the porous tar above. It will be plenty
not to meet, whenever I go out, the random
knives into my eye on the sidewalks,
the random onset of blindness, the lying
waiting to be scraped up. Plenty
not to feel the noise of the sirens
screeching nearer as relief. It will be plenty
and undeserved just to be alone
and the least known beneficiary.

Letter to Breton

Breton à l'avant de soi

Dear André, I'm sorry,
it's hard for me to see what's here. I want
your super
stition, more precisely real
than inquiry after causes. Your great
standpoint. Your standing over
against, to watch. I want
your glass wolf who is coming and roams the plazas
while women in the houses around
lightly touch
translucent curtains to look out
in expectation. Your locust
mounted on a fast horse
and bending into the wind which
striking her in the face carries her forward
floating to deliver
the urgent mail. I would have sent the news
faster with a phone call. But then my letter
would have been in vain. Unless you cross
vast distances, all distance, in your body, in pain,
exulting, nothing can be
delivered. The message stays
buried in a message: *Hello. Hello? Are you*
still there? What do you take me for?
Who? What's happened
to you? Did they kill you?
Are you there? There is only world
in a kiss.

On a Thought of Juan Ramón Jiménez

And what difference does all of it make
if as fire we can consume
each pain and sorrow—O passion—in a star...?

And what difference does it make if my woods
are cut and burning
if I arrive as fire in pure space;
that my oceans, that my lake,
that my narrow adolescent river
sparkle with deception,
infused poison shining like water in the water reflecting heaven
where the razed oaks once leaned over?

If I'm a rose
now without stem or earth
because my memory is a greater stem
transforming all it conveys,
as it feeds me from my former life all fused into consciousness—
and being is my true earth now, my only soil?

If I remain then unchanging
blossoming,
what difference does it make—the homeland
I leave that freely promised me once it was
just one step from Eden...
Leave it on the roadside,
a dank knot, a rind, rot, garbage in action?

What difference does it make,
the unemployed wife and husband dead
of an overdose behind their steering wheel,

their two toddlers crying in the back seat
of their old Honda ticking by a ditch
in my Arcady?

What difference does it make that I have nothing to say
to the one true radicalism—
yours, Juan Ramón:
beauty alone, the root and the flower
that are the fruit—nothing to say
to your rightness but these contrasts and comparisons
between horror lived
and the perfecting of the endless desire?

In the Motet of Mondonville

In the motet of Mondonville
where the ladies' voices rise to gloria
and tarry there, in that dwelling, so liquid and aureate,
is a poet's anguish and failure to draw out
the quickly passing word to its long hidden extent,
its two or three syllables to their endless number,
the letters of those sounds to their single sign,
something like the sun but the centre
of more than the sun is, maybe of all, and with a kinder
warmth, a ferocity more human-blooded,
a warmer dust, more breathable, a gentler cloud,
a single cloud, one drop, a messenger of rain
falling on the tents of hell,
sizzling on the skins, appearing as three strangers at the tent flap
in the desert evening. The ladies' voices are the simplicity
of the three strangers' greeting that brings water
to the burnt eyes fastened with wooden screws
to the minutiae of impossibility.
O those women, I can't see them, but I hear
them tossing their heads in sprightly dance
on a wooded lakeshore. Flowers!—
they're flowers, as the ancient compliment says they are,
they want to be flowers. Now they rise
from their graves and aspire. They see me,
they're unafraid. We send sex
to women in flowers, as the great poet said:
red flowers, blue, yellow, white, purple, red,
and we hang waiting for their reply. Gloria. Maybe
she loves me not, she loves me,
but who am I to know? Serpent of magic healing
and betrayal, hang

listening prehensile glistening
in the curved boughs of the tree that gave you birth
that comes from above and below.

The Sun

The sun when it first came to be,
a spark of a distant explosion
and throwing off other sparks and extraneous matter—the veils,
the touchless particles, of smoke—and spinning, spinning,
the sun
had no idea that later
its nature would be divined
by dervishes guiding great ships into the sea,
gyroscopes guiding great ships across the night.

The sun said I am totally consumed
in my burning and my rotation.
I send out light...I think,
but can't see. If I have produced anything,
if I have had any merit,
I will not know it. It
will not be me
that credits it.

O sun,
first blind man, first saint
compelled to holiness by misery,
first wanderer
in the vast burning plains
of the vast frigidity,
founder of our brief
immemorial tradition.

Hearing from You

O my belovèd monster, I can't say
that when I first saw you I was stricken
and filled with fear, or astonishment,
or horror and disgust, or awe
at immensity, beauty—awe that these things were real
and did exist somewhere and were greater
than I was ever told,
had ever dreamed. I was only shocked
so much that I was nothing but the shock. I was a splinter
flying in the explosion of your coming.
A streak of that fire. Flying
from you, a part of you. Then I lay
on the ground later
and recalled, after a long or short not knowing
anything, that I am you. Still in this quiet
motionlessness, where the birds, to my stunned awakening,
are brighter and sweeter, fluttering,
whispering, as soon I too will again
start doing, I am being
thrown here from you.

No Longer

Now I've reached where it is no longer
possible to live with you
another fifty years on earth. I know it
but don't feel it. I feel us together
doing what we do. Tomorrow, what will be
in the news? Will anything be new, finally?
We can't wait to see.
The garden we planned and worried
and sometimes halfway made—what will occur
to that? What fresh ideas will it get?
We saw it crossed by all the glories
and storms of the sky and ocean—these were almost
its only flowers, not much came from the ground—
and other times it was crushed
by a mudslide the colour of dullness.
Gather up the fragments, that nothing may be lost.
Cease to live just in the flickers of the mind.
Now I've reached where it's no longer possible
to be with you another fifty years
on earth. I know it but don't feel it. My feeling is
that we go on as ever. My conclusion: What
is "possible"? What is "no longer"?

Quibble with Hegel

The oak is an acorn
and blesses its origin: this oak, standing alone,
giving bunches—centuries—of acorns that drop to sleep
beneath it and are lightly nibbled
by squirrels, or collected first, some polished
and strung on threads, by children.
The cap and the glans once separated,
the cap is a little hat
for a small fingertip, or, turned over,
a little coracle bound for mystic Ireland
across a sidewalk puddle. This craft
is getting nowhere. In it, the studious
gaze of the children kneeling by the water
is the holy monk.

WHEN I WAS A CHILD

When I Was a Child

When I was a child
and had nothing to do
but read and wander
the streets and railroad tracks
and stream banks of Niles,
I said to God:
If you've killed the gods,
the way they tell me,
I'll never run into anyone
here to love me. No,
they're just shy, came an answer,
and maybe you are one
and with them right now.
Walking lonely and happy
along the ties.
Watching out from the long rise
of the right-of-way across
the beautiful scrub
of flowering weeds where the meadowlarks
and flying grasshoppers
hide and rise and the mustard bushes
flower to gold.
Happy in the quiet
of the walk. Too much
a godhead to see
or care
it never gets anywhere.
I always got back home
on time more or less,
more or less late
to the angry parents.

But I'd arrived. I'd found
the walk and would again
tomorrow, while it was still summer,
or in the snow or rain,
afternoon or the first stars.
But I didn't see it like that:
"journey," "arrive."
I would just set out
every day through Niles
where I was
a child.

When Chappie Got Out

When Chappie got out from his ten years,
having taken the rap or fall (as we actually used to say,
being fools) for some higher-ups, he went right back
to driving his cab. Which meant
piloting the occasional old lady to the grocery store
or up to the bus station in Warren. Mostly
just sitting around, parked on State,
cap on head, brown-burnt arm with thick cover
of black and curly hairs, just like mine,
skin baking still deeper on the frame of the rolled-down
driver's-side window. Leaning to look up at you
for a six-word conversation. He would've returned
to running numbers if they'd still wanted him.
He had had some pocket money back then
though he was always just a weasel. Murray McLauchlan
sings lovingly of an old farmer
with "a face like a shoe." Chappie
had a face like the imprint of a shoe on the front
of an unrecognizable corpse's head. Always smiling.
Not making the best of things but imitating
making the best of things
for his own edification.
What did he do when he went home at night?
I saw him at home. It was like
when you turn off the lawnmower and put it in the shed
and you close the door
and it's sitting in there.

When I Was a Child

When I was a child it was clear
the stones are alive. Plunging in tall grasses,
almost lost to each other, we always
were meeting them in the new trails
each of us crushed, invisible to one another
but near, calling out, smelling the faint
sweetness in the afternoon drift of light. A stone
was no companionable creature like the wary
groundhog or blue jay watching us calmly far off,
the impassible grasshopper caught, waiting, staring
on our palms. The stones live another way, all stones
the same stone life, so strange—the dark ones, wet,
we stood on in the creek, the sandy ones
we tried to hurl across, the ones that hurt me,
the sandstone cliff, its tilted narrow path
of smooth stone where one day I slid and fell.

The learning of the life of stones
goes on. Later I've met
faint images of it flickering
in ideas: the hierarchy
of spirit. Or the physics
of tiny worlds—grains that wander
separate, each one chained down
to every other. No matter
where they lie or travel, each blown mote
an imperial center
never to be moved. I've admired
these poignant speculations, poor
forays into the first beaches
and forest fringes of

back when I was a child
and it was clear
the stones are alive.

I Know I Was

When I was a child
selfish, all-grasping
in my forgetting all the time
to come in,
get clean, I know I was
remembering to run
after the hovering
beetle. The gods that don't
exist, as people call it, moved—
the mauve cloud, the stars
and their cousins the spring
beauties in the grass. Dim vanishings
into elderberry thickets in fruit
in humid chilly fog, August mornings.
August noons, as naked as
Deborah and Diane and I were
running into the woods, gods
with us. If that runnel
doesn't flow now, such that it is not
and it was not, then this is not
the world. But where I was
a selfless child
is a world. I do believe
I was a river free
to know how it goes,
to flow, sparkle, dull, rage, and cry
out for terror, for balking, for no reason
but the sky is crying. Wandering drew
and the gods watched the shapes
of world appearing. We rounded
corners and pushed aside green veils,
parted thicknesses and disappeared

inside. We're gone, Diane. Brightness
and shadow in here, ripples in reflection,
rocks and clouds murmured in all
that passed down the current around
the bend beyond seeing. Here
it is. It talks—leaps
of a fish the eye would never
quite catch. This all was a
music, so that my small hands, when
handed the keys and a book, corrected
Mozart to the melody
we had in mind. So then the heavy-
breasted metronome came to stand
above, harden and speed
my fingers, shout, hit
my donkey-springbok knuckles
and the bare backsides
of my palms with the edge of
the ruler. New music, the ennoblement
of the measured, fled,
a freshet, in the wet woods. I do believe
it plays out here,
a spring with power to decide
to be alone and sad
and frightened to go home
and still to be
the spring.

Seeds People Thoughts

Elm seeds—pale green whole notes—softly
land on the prairie of dark sharp greens:
the lawn. The same way thoughts
land on the white expanses of a notebook.
Except the seeds arrive at the grass, a lot
of thoughts vanish unnoted before
they reach their ground. Are they lost goods
or are they saved somewhere
or were they already nothing
when they became nothing? O profusion,
gift of god or image
of god's vengeance on the world...I will think thoughts
are the transformation of memory
from museum to life. With the red and ochre birds,
with the blue and golden flies, they pass
into the air. Other ones light on paper and fall through
onto shelves and are hidden there,
some in never being found,
some in being seen and passed by: birds and flies
of the unplumbed forest, of legend, of a place
real but most of it only imagined
by someone going down a path through some region
of thick forest. Thoughts lost, unvisited
like the old people remembered in that they are stored
somewhere, remaining where they are for a while,
a memento from a past life, childhood—a secret
almost unintentionally kept
secret. And then you might see them one day as if
you had never seen them, as if a star
finally glimpsed again after years
is a new star.

You Don't Know

You don't know. You never have gone anywhere,
they said. You have no travels. You haven't known
women and men and customs, haven't seen
their countries—mountains stony and low
or vast, inaccessible, covered with dawn and snow.
Their villages threatened or resting near faithful treacherous tides.
You can't twist and stick in their strange tongues.
Your farthest trip was from the chair to the door,
across the little creek by the bridge to the store
to the packaged bread in cellophane with red and gold balloons.
Yes, but wind in the treetops was the ocean.
Was sometimes the gale, the divine gale that tore
and half-wrecked the very sea. Its gentle fall
soughing was the wave-action in the middle ocean,
fallen asleep, and surf's fall on endless sand.
Under the ridge a spring trickled from vertical rock,
darkening the shale. In those woods was a huge boat
beached and breached. The scent of violets under oak
leaves of last winter. I was little, I was dreaming
of righting it, caulking, painting, getting a crew
of the other children, getting it to the stream
just visible over there past the dark shade of noon,
the tangle of jewelweed and nightshade along the bank,
launching it, sailing God knows where—everywhere
while above me was the far-travelled oriole singing.

How at Home

I'm sick of addressing you, night,
you never answer me.
Night stretched and yawned
in the infinity of its loving terror and boredom
hearing me and not hearing me.
How at home I was!
—in the huge silent house alone, so huge
it was a world—mine: a fate of exposure
on stone or sand, adventure of being lost
in scrub or woods, or on a long rocky coast
or soft beach of a shoreless ocean. It was empty,
full of crepitations of creatures
I never saw, and sparse-bodied motives in the grass,
and way over there the glow
of cities and rising moons.

Adolescence

I

Was this dark hollow
always inside me
or was it suddenly created, maybe last night,
in my sleep? Created by what—by me?

2

Is it a hollow—like a well? It might be an empty
road at night that you see
having come to the crest of a hill. Is it
a dark? What's down there,
vaguely glimmering? There's no light in the sky.
Maybe it's a vast land all around
a sloping path that canters and curvets
into and through it. Maybe it's a cliff's edge
above a motionless grey ocean—or above
a vast splendour you can't reach
except by falling and dying there.

3

The peace of being stopped
here—where?—in moist darkness.
But it can't be peace—my heart bucks,
it loses any rhythm, all expectation.
Expectation turns to fear
of ending—but it is peace

to be stopped here in the moist
erupting darkness.

4

With this dark,
yearning appeared.
From this hollow I turned into
yearning across to you.

5

I used to want the big people
to quit shouting. I could see
everything in our house would be happy
with just a desire, like mine,
for it to be. Was that the seed
of yearning? A seed—the movement
to you
splits my heart
like roots split the ground,
and it branches out
as my veins. My fingers
quiver and whisper, my eyes glint.

6

When I was a child
I found things
nobody wanted—places
where they'd leave me

alone till they wanted me. A scrap of woods,
a great forest to me
until the hurled voices of where-have-
you-got-to-now
penetrated it easily.
Or a book, in the library
or in the house,
that no one read, O tearful
night, O great
star, O helpless...
but I was
in it reading.

7

When I was a child
alone, there came an age of being without
even the scrap of a place
that I had known, the book
that I hid. I couldn't remember anymore
being alone...couldn't recall that I was still
alone. That was the second loneness. With the shout
of put-that-down-come-
out-of-there-you-
good-for-nothing, they had abolished even, even
in my mind
my minuscule
wilderness of patches.

8

When I was a child, there came a time
when I looked up and around. No more playing now,
no more swinging my fist
in soft blows, all that my pretty rage could do in the lost
endearing kittenhood. I find myself
big now. One of the big people. The fist could kill.
I've already seen it
cut open cheeks, break ribs,
and later, washing my wounds, I wondered
at the mirror and the knuckles. It could kill
in the exasperation of desire
readily, with an effort so minor to its strength,
it would go as little felt
as a whim. I have to
keep apart, I have to never be
one of the big people, I have to not
use what I am
or find it some other use.

9

Yes
here
is the fulfillment of
when I was
a child. Childhood finds itself
eternal from this place
of terror of peace. I love you
as if I were a lava flow. Don't betray me
by fright at the surging
repulsiveness overshrouding

the old kitten, at my paralysis the core
of a motionless night
looming, don't fail me
by being just
another being.
This world has become
your standing
across from, against, before. Receive
with heat
to keep alive.

The Dusk

A child is in the house alone.
The other howling snatching children
and the big people all are gone.
To tell him what and where he must
be at, to shout, now there is no one.
He could shout himself, if he should want.
Now he could break and run,
stampede, across the rooms, upstairs and down.
No hands that grab and squeeze him to the bone
and stop him are anywhere around.
No threat surrounds him now and towers
over him in the seeming peaceful
murmurs and silences of giants and gangs.
The thought to yell and charge starts dying,
almost, in him. He sits quiet.
There is a gold and purple twilight
in the window, with lightning bugs
beginning to light, afloat
in the fir tree in the yard.
The house is locked and neat,
the wastes he was charged with taking out
are disposed, the stars are up above
the roof, slow turning, soft and hard.
The dusk of struggle keeps increasing.
He grows the knowledge of the good.

House

It was a house plummeting through the night.
At last I had a home. A place
to stay, my own, a different place
from the hideous roofless pesterings, the appearances
and disappearings that never let me alone.

It was a house collapsing into itself.
When I'd swept all the floors, caulked the cracks,
dusted the picture frames and rubbed the cheap
glasses brighter than crystal, nothing needed
to be fixed ever again. I could walk from view to view,
and any shifting of a figurine
was only for a slightly other beauty.

It was a house all alone in a woods and meadow
among unpopulated hills ringed in by cliffs
snowy in the summers. Twenty steps to the door
and I could shut away the sirens
across the lawn outside, the rusted knives
and needles in gutters, the shouts and threats
or starving-dog indifference of the beggars.

It was a house mine alone
where I could think that if the one I love
ever came home...I would know at last
how to be with her. In that house all my old failure
was just a happy moment of expecting
her soon return in the great continuance
of our being together.

It was a house where no one but me can come—

if they came to see whether I'm dead or asleep, they'd find
the breeze in the open doors, the white
curtain stirring, and a cleanly un-
disquieting rind.

The Memoirs of A. F. Moritz

I was born a happy boy
and grew to be a happy man,
joked and laughed, and only from time to time
glimpsed myself in a mirror
or an eyeball, was given a gaze
from out there beyond me, a look gone in a flash,
maybe a dream—I hope so—and saw
an ugly fool. And so, two things. My resolve
always to thrust my chin and hairline forward,
tuck in my nose, walk with toes directed
straight forward, not splayed,
stand up straight, remember to quit sighing out loud—resolutions
that I can often practise for a quarter hour non-stop
before forgetting them in slopped distraction.
They are exercises that I can't put together.
So complicated they are, my whole intelligence,
which is considerable, can only make me elegant
for brief intervals and pathetically,
theoretically, like playing tennis
out of a book. The second thing: a person is supposed
to gain self-acceptance with age.
This has not been my experience. The old first shock of
astonishment and pain has gone on every day
becoming more: more the meaning
of a revelation, so a fresh crushing, a new stab.
I imagine that near-death, when it comes to me,
will be the last defeat of all effort to look
and act like a human being. The final slump
into slack-jaw, stink, and general
lack of grace. And another thing,
one I didn't learn, it was born with me,

it seems. I know how to live in one second the whole life
of a bitter hermit, a castaway
presumed to be drowned in a wreck
decades ago—I know how to live
that chosen, fated, accidental isolation,
those slow years of solace in being unseen and quiet,
all in a single afternoon, a single hour. You see
me with you. I'm alone in cave above the sea, cursing myself,
staring out at the endless beauty and storms,
and I get tired of it and fall asleep,
and wake up by magic in this city of yours,
back before you know I'm gone.

The Crossing

How can this lonely crossing be
so crowded? You're alone.
Nothing except a winter-straw moon.
But bicycles, pushcarts, children's wagons
keeping coming in, swiping each other, gone. Cars,
tanks, and sedan chairs draped in pale green samite
with white tassels and purfling. Yellow-and-black
taxicabs avid with advertisements. Lovers stroll,
blind in each other, with the motion of a new
runnel after May rain, and how do they pass right through?
Why don't they have to dodge the protest demonstration,
the fife and drum corps, the six young drunks
shouting and taking up all the space,
children eeling in and out
everywhere, old dodderers
pausing at the angles of walls,
turning their bodies, talking to the plaster,
the businesspeople barging into
lunch bistros, the delivery men wheeling racks
and crates across the stuffed sidewalks
towards the alleys and loading bays?

The crowds take up the earth. There is no earth
but comings-and-crossings here from the whole disc
of the horizon, the whole sphere of space.
And yet you don't have to mind them
any more than the lovers do. You're alone.
Alone and going home
from a failed chance. You come
to the intersection. A simple cross: two old
minor highways meeting at right angles

at 2 a.m. in November fields. The usual
square of asphalt where the two are one
for a moment. Silence of little wind
in the mummy cornstalks. Cold that is almost warm
through motionlessness. The simplest, emptiest,
dreariest of crossings. You were let out here.
November 1966. No money left. Four hundred miles
from your room. The moon, slow sliding cloud-film,
no cars or trucks, no house in sight
in the form of small lights across the wide fields.
You intend to, you will, pick up a ride here
to Richmond, Indiana, not far off.

Pawnshop Row

The pawnshops are thinning out and pawnshop row
soon will be all condo towers, I suppose.
My heart is dented, hurt, silently
moved. The huge tuba-like instrument
of blackening never-polished silver
and unpressed valves, not claimed
for decades on its throne of velvet
in the much-bypassed window
till it has become no longer a good for sale
or to be redeemed
but an emblem
is my heart.

This Is You

As the city spreads and closes in,
the only things left living
are humans. And these diminish
to nothing but gestures they still can make
themselves make. People who don't exist,
not so much as in the mind's wish,
the heart's imagination, let alone on earth,
until they lift a finger by a labour of
the will. People only there
from the moment they wave a hand
they decide to lift to greet
the nonexistent others. Others like flashes,
like scarce motions of air. Others unknown
until a wave salutes them. Not here
until with a motion of salutation
they were sketched. Then from less than ashes
they get up, fill themselves in,
and live.

Looking around, they find themselves
torn between gratitude and horror.

There still is a world. This one, hidden
in the material city spreading wide,
closing in. This is you, crushed
field of faint gestures to things—motions—
infinite as a stirring too tiny,
too stifled, to be heard—bodies
that are names only
just now being made up, never yet said.

THERE IS STILL

There Is Still

There's still a jar on a hill in Tennessee
because he thought there was,
he said there was.
There's still a witch in the wood
and a spring of God or a spring
of a prophet of a god
and still a leman crying over the corpse of her knight
beside a woodland well,
though the wood is gone. These propositions
are equal to the beauty of a tree
but not to the tree. That tree creates
propositions like seeds, as seeds, as it does
seeds. Or once it did
create them. And now they flitter this way:
they flitter down. The witch seems
gone with the forest
but for the glow of her,
remaining—glow that humans called the body,
once upon a time: something that shimmers
outward to them from a shape, giving them eyes,
ears, and fingertips, giving them something
to occupy, to come occupy
their undiscovered hollers. But I have lost
my way here. The witch, seeming gone, her glow
so distant, many are torn
to personate her false repute, monster,
in alleys and cellars, paths
and valleys of the empty
argot of psychology: the psychopath
is absent affect. Having killed
and devoured, it stands

in the forest waters, blinking
like a fish, staring like a bird...no! Not
forest, not water. No fish likeness,
bird likeness. It is standing alone,
like a herm of salt, a fragment
of an I-beam thrown from the explosion
to land here and stick upright
in the sand. Among these warehouses
of hermits, sorcerers, bandits, heroes,
vindictive paynims, Cyclopes,
driven mad by love, wandering
horses of dead warriors, along straight rows
dusty in the former
industrial town: everything was torn down
but the grid. We are living, slipping,
on the graphite-powder back
of a treacherous vast gigantoboa or plesiosaur
drifting peacefully, sometimes lazily
stirring a fin or ring
in the sea of boundless night
but it can't plunge and drown us:
there's nothing but surface to this ocean,
everywhere is surface, the one direction that exists
is up and out. And it is at dead center:
nowhere but here to go. But as I was saying,
that tree we cut down, which is all trees, produces
propositions like seeds and equal to
the beauty of trees, but not
to the tree. And from this mated inequality
comes veneration, restitution,
restoration, preservation—oh, all the muses
of our day, lonely, dancing, chanting, stomping
soft roseate feet, trembling their breasts,
giving their thighs and climbing, tumbling

hair to the hands of the air,
their hips to eyes, lips to ears
until the spell suggested
by what they fear to forget, almost forget,
brings back the ground to their soles,
warmth for their passing hands. They inspire,
friendship they bring,
bone and flesh they bring back,
body they restore, life they restore,
god they remake, for their leader—formerly dead
young man, old man
wandering absently somewhere
in the lack
of the trees he used
to tend in the evenings.

The Nature of Thought

And we are more than ready,
I sang, *to enter the bedchamber*
where the angel of seventeen years
eternally grows more perfectly
seventeen. Good old poetry!
We are young and then
we grow more and more
no longer what we are. And the whole
future becomes the beautiful
vision of restitution
in perfection. But what about the ones,
the thought comes, who never were
what they are? What about
an old one for whom the divine
magic of restoration
to the perfect year, more perfected,
would be to be thrust back
into an earlier length of the present
creeper of deformation, hideousness,
despair? Maimed body, all he was ever
given. What's to be said about him?
Him who hates and laments
youth for a good reason. Nothing.
No one could have the great
gentleness, the knowledge, and the right
to say anything about him. In the world
there is no nothing, but in the world
of chattering questioning there comes
a nothing when the question
truly appears. What about? leads on
to no right, which leads to nothing,

silence, and the thought,
“only dwell with,” “only cherish,”
if you can, you who blessed yourself
as too brave to be squeamish. In
that thought, you heard at last
all that thought is. Dwell with,
cherish, talk about
work, needlepoint, baseball,
the heat of the day, the cool evening,
the smell of the rain
on grass and dirt in the sweet darkness
beyond the porch of the institution.

To the Unending

You are an upright statue fallen,
old man—or maybe not so old, just toothless.
I passed you each morning on your corner,
one knee folded up to your chest, one leg
stretched out, barring the sidewalk,
your red paper begging cup
cupped between them at the point of your sex
glimpsed in the sagged grey crotch
of your sweatpants full of holes. You're slumped now
onto your side and face, one ear
to the concrete. A few passersby are noticing,
up ahead there, and starting to come back,
touch you, poke you, and talk, you soft statue,
to your stillness. To this corner you came and sat
no one knows how long, relentlessly making yourself
ever more yourself, the way a great poet makes his mind.
Day after day, remorseless, sick, tired,
making yourself your work, you sat
observing, absorbing, returning every ankle
and hubcap that passed your eyes. Only and true
statue possible of man and his name,
including every line, real and ideal,
of the human male in your total form,
delineated to its end, that is to say,
to the unending.

The Path

You told me you were on a path—
a path, you called it—and frantic to take
all other paths. Frantic to have taken
all others you'd ever noticed. As you went,
you crossed intersections, bypassed side roads
and heads of trails, maybe human, maybe animal,
maybe nothing at all, just vegetable gaps.
How anxious you were not to be accused
of having not seen everything that is
essential. You trembled with torturing
eagerness at the maw of every turn-off.
But if you ever took one, you said it was
the same. It was the path you were on
and it went along bypassing many others,
filling your memory with roads
to who knows what—nightmares, lands
of dream. Every way you went,
it was the path, and around it: the clustering
of shadows, something like dense woods
beginning to stir in a night wind,
memories of alley-mouths, openings
half-barred by branches and leaves...

The Living Fleet Eternity of Thought

“The living fleet eternity of thought”:
only survivor from lines the small hours brought.
Last night I sang the whole poem in my brain,
solely as a form of thinking. Down the drain
it went, as though I’d flushed and watched it eddy
into sleep and the undared darkness of my body.
It was a gift to me that should have been written
down, and kept. For this it had been given.
How I wish now I’d done as I was bidden.
I woke up the next day. What had I got?
That I was here while what I’d received was not—
except as the living fleet eternity of thought.
So morning tried what tiredness had disdained
and I wrote this—the bit that has remained.

A Blue Bicycle

I

This poet died twice. His work was known a little
just in our town for a short while, and then
nowhere at all. His death remained a fact
to almost no one, although gradually,
year by year, some lovers of poetry did hear
that the person corresponding to some poems
they'd heard once from the microphone in a bar
and could remember the existence, not the words, of,
was no more. Others also recalled the poems
once in a while, not thinking to wonder why
they never saw the man—if he was dead or only
alive but elsewhere. In the latter case, you could say,
this poet had not died even once. Elsewhere or dead:
what's the difference? So let's call it elsewhere.

2

This poet died once. His work remained unknown
except to some friends and frequenters of the bars
where poetry, including his, used to be read aloud.
Where, over years, they'd watched him getting poorer
and poorer, more and more weird. I used to see him
peddling his old, stiff, rusted bicycle, still bearing
some flecks of blue enamel, along College Street
in the rain in a dirty trench coat—same coat for years,
decades. He developed theories on famous disasters
and was writing an endless novel, they say—I don't know
about what or if anyone did. And then he died.
I heard it long afterwards from his friends. I was
a peripheral one. And sometimes in a bar I still
hear him mentioned the way you mention a thing
you can't see, touch, or remember, yet you know it
as a certain hole in your world. His poems now
were nothing but him along with his blue bicycle,
raincoat, and the room he must have had somewhere
with doubtless reams of more poems: he was dead.
No one I know knows where the poems went.

Survivor

They say to me,
"You are the last, true,
but you are—there is—one."
Yes, but that is the same thing
as what I said: "We
are none."

The Allegory of the Cave

Once there was a garbagy shallow cave
where some of us sat, backs to the mouth,
and on the back wall we watched shadows created
by the sun outside (when, rarely, it was day)
and things passing along out there. A wise man
appeared behind us and told us all we had
were shadows, that we were failing to turn
and look behind us and see things and the light.
He said we were bound down there and first of all
by our own stupidity, our satisfaction.
Some time after he'd been ignored and had left,
there was a stir. Gradually, they all decided.
They did turn around. They got up and went out.
Alas for them. The cave shadows had already been
things, just like the trees and the busy people, and the sun
they all got in the way of to make shadows.
The ex-cave-dwellers now spent all their time
eating honey, patting bottoms, looking at birds,
things like that: more of them, more colourful
than shadows, but still, things. The vast rondure
of the day was their new cave, and the greater vault
of the night and constellations was another cave
and the much greater sphere of their deduction
and speculation on the farther invisible stars
and their actions and history, and all the skies and planets
within a drop of water, and all the skies and planets
within each one of those, was another cave
and so forth. Me, I stayed in the cave.
The shadows—let me say "the shadow"
for simplicity's, I mean accuracy's, sake—
the shadow wasn't much. I was poor

but it was there with me. I was like a man
with a loved pet, let's say a cat. I was a man
with a mute visitant: the shadow couldn't or wouldn't
respond as I wanted to demand, and it even would
relapse at times into identity with the peace of night,
but it moved and purred and stayed. I had a friend.

In the Norway Maple of July

In the Norway maple of July,
already a passage of red leaves.

Still almost a boy, I used to go far across town
to a job in a miserable office
and always at a certain stop, into the bus
a beautiful woman would climb and sit down
across the aisle. Her hair especially
engraved itself within me: black waves and curls,
a mass, a perfect casual shape, breakers of liquid jet—
but all combed through with wires of startling white.
Straggles of shocking white writhed everywhere
in the soft abundant blackness. And yet
she was at most twenty-eight. I watched her pass
day after day with amazement. I kept my eyes
a secret from her, not to disturb. Was she a girl
in her longing heart? Didn't she see, just out of bed,
the same mystery in the mirror
that I saw, as she arranged it, as she had to—life
had given her that task? A severe and overwhelming,
alien beauty, a prophecy, a presence,
a temptation to regret. Unfathomable vision, for me
everlasting remembrance. Now total white
may long have overflowed the mysterious veins,
their motionless curving, and engulfed the black light
around her head. Now
she may well be dead.

Householder

I dwell in possibility—that's the name
of my true house. As true as this one
with windows, walls, and ceilings, and a roof
sealing me off from the too pointed gaze
of my love, the sky. A house fit for my body,
and fit for my spirit, which is a body too,
though you can't see it.

But I don't truly have a house.
I have a parallelepiped,
a sort of stretched-out cube of space
sketched on a plan in an intellect
and traced with wires and kept in place
up in the air about two hundred feet
by being stacked with more just like it. A box
just right apparently for a featherless biped,
though birds are kept in wood and wire shapes
not unlike—more fanciful, usually—and tigers
used to be, before the enlightenment that set them free
to roam a little in a little greenery
kept somewhere in the city
and to lie in the sun under a tree
before returning to the feeding tray
well-known in the evening.

Yet I do dwell—ancient word
in which there is a hut and beside it a well
into the dust, rock, water, mineral fire
and surrounding darkness
of blessèd rest—down through all that
into the flesh, felt again to be

true longing, house
with its body and soul—possibility.

Liking to Be a Tree

It's true that I would like to be a tree
but false that a tree does not hurt anyone.
A tree's a shoot that sprang where a single ray
reached the ground from the leaf cover. Sun-fed,
it alone, from the litter of seeds and the saplings
thin as grasses, lived. Titanic, it plugs
that mothering gap of light with its green arches,
more perfectly strangling with a deeper dimness
all but lips of fungi. For the traveller:
a warm empty quiet of old twigs
decaying in the shadowy openness
among boles and snags, and the natural
benches waiting: trunks fallen years ago,
shaped, softened, burnished by the craftsman
of the air, who never finishes adding touches.

It's a tree that, chosen to stand over a house,
will crack in half from age or lightning, fall
and shatter walls, human limbs, a life,
two lives—a child, a mother, one crushed, one left.
Then the enraged avengers come, too late
as always ensuring it won't happen again.
The chainsaw screeches righteousness.
The tree's remainder lies in slices. All
that's left behind is the flat irregular circle
of the stump's face, a giant's table board
to children—first, a-glitter with freshness, smooth,
and then dark-varnished once the seasons turn
its crime and death to legend. No one ever
pulls it up. No one comes with an axe
and chops it out—chops wedge by wedge to beneath

ground level and covers it over: that talent
or that gumption lost. How many afternoons
of my adolescence chopping out stumps...
Stubborn task, engine of pride in strength,
competence, endurance: swinging the axe,
pausing to breathe and sweat bare-chested. No,
it isn't so that a tree hurts no one. Better be
a slender stem and flower of a white clover
in a meadow we used to visit. Then, love, you
would have a clover flower against the sunset
in the shot glass on our windowsill.

Would Have Taken Up

I rise, the sun too.
It passes over and I work.
I work and it passes farther.
Stay, sun, stay!
I'm not finished yet!
But if I keep working
and try to make it
remain today
till this work is complete,
I'll ruin tomorrow
with lack of sleep.
I'll get up late. Then nothing
can be done. No—I
disagree. Sleep is given
to me as a personal night.
I can put it
wherever I want. I can commit
every sin. But no, it's time now
to put things down
and go to bed.
What got done?
You get up, a few
strokes of the pen,
the day's over. Also there was
a hurried letter
to a...friend, I'll call her.
I was so pressed I felt
I couldn't spare her
anything longer. O if I'd written her
what I wanted, everything
that composed itself

in my heart, a sung world
as glorious as this one
in a moment of thought,
it would have taken up
my whole day. Sweetly.
And then: sleep. It would have
taken up
all my life.

THE TAWER

The Tawer

I could survive because a vast many of things
came to be wanted and I could find a place
in the processes of making them—the same reason
my family and my kind were born at all.
A class of people who never were before
the machines, big crowds, and cities. We emerged
from nowhere, from the new need: were a teratoid
to the early orders: peasants, nobles, priests,
the guilds—masons, jongleurs: the old humans,
who'd grown out of the meristem over ages:
mushroom gatherers; fishermen. Our industry
was no longer a virtue. Our plants did not grow.
Me, I lived on the river because my work
took water. I was a dyer sometimes, a tanner,
a tawer—rinsed salts and alum, urine and dung
in the dead stream we'd killed. My stinking trade
was kept outside the old gates. But still the currents
of poison seeped through town, till you buried them
two hundred years later. My river's just a part now
of your drains, there under you. Your bowels.

The river of my day became your sewer,
beautifully roofed with the drives and walks you take
to the new museum. And so seldom does it stink
at all, I could easily have rhymed it with "ewer,"
or contrariwise, made of myself an angry novel like those
that flowed long after my time from Monsieur Zola.
But I don't want you thinking this was our "story,"
that everyone has a "story," even me—that everyone
possesses or is possessed by an end. If I'm a story
to God and this exalts me, neither I nor anyone

knew. And least of all you, you little nullifidians
with your littler and ever littler piece of the profit
my long gone life was macerated into.

You'll find the trades of tawer, dyer, tanner
written beside the names of those guillotined
after the insurrection. Horse dealer, smith,
thresher, day labourer...Their only marks:
name and work. The one way they had to write
had been the barricades' three-day festival and fall.

Myself, I lived in a place with no insurrection,
no festival. I could survive, because
things came to be wanted by vast manys
and I found a place in making them. I never heard
that there was an insurrection somewhere else
in any of the years I lived. That Monsieur Rousseau
had once made books that were fuses, I did not know
till I was dead and thus knew everything,
as the dead do. And so I know that I
am your equal—you eager inheritor
of inventions, processes, and all the nets
they join into, wire vines crowding down all woods.
You receiver of all the goods and so
of all the evils. You living presence of the pain
of people now dying long ago in the mines,
in the works of acid, lime, and mercury.
You in your Jaguar and your elsewhere dying out
jaguars—in the light of this death of mine I know
that all is well and still
you owe me my life. You owe me my life on earth,
which was to be happiness in clean mornings
by the sparkling clear ripples under the trees
of my treeless congealed stream. If now you ever

do anything for any instant but weep blood
from your eyes in the strain of trying to discover
how you can give me back the gentle dawns
you owe me—I who've been dead two hundred years—
you're a fool and a murderer.

Choice

When prison was imposed,
I chose it. Then the warden hated me,
for he was on the inside and I was out.
No matter how much he ate
in his continent-wide apartment
above the watchtowers, no matter how much he drank
forgetting where ambition had got him,
no matter how long his vacations
in legendary capitals, where he could enjoy statues
dissolving into the water rising in the canals,
he was on the inside and I was out.
I won't make you a picture of the lashings
and rackings his sleek guards gave me then—
it would be indecent literature. But by comparison
with my red carcass, the torturers' beauty looked
pathetic, and my disjointed shape
created in their former satisfaction
what is termed astonishment. It's the sight
you can't look away from, can't even want
to look away from, though you close your eyes,
not knowing if this new fascination of yours
is some magnetic horror
or the fulfilling of a hope you scarcely dreamed
until now, when you are watching it be answered
under your murdering hands.

The Tradition

He descended to the dead,
wrapped an old towel around his waist,
cooked the soup,
manhandled the huge tin vat to the trestle table,
ladled into bowls,
handed to hands,
listened to lappings and suckings,
watched sad eager lips.
So my grandmother did the same.

Interior Peace

Here I'm happy
under the peaceful moon
between half and full, sailing so slow
it takes an hour to cross the inches
between the seventieth storeys of two towers.
I'm happy down here and also up there
where my eyes live on the moon and with her—
with the moon as science tells me definitively she is not
but she is. Soon there will be camps
and mines up there and my soul
will sing the aubade of the moon
beside the rhythm of drills, just like
it does now in the Arabian deserts
and stunted Texas, smallest state
of mind in the union. Here I'm happy
and my heart in my eyes
lives in the immense, while others enviously,
vengefully prove how it can't be so,
and in their constantly dismantled and constructed place
children sleep against the walls of thin marble
veneer, and I step over them, here in the region
of big companies and drug zombies,
pain and arrogance squeezing the neck of my peace,
shaking its spine, shouting: Spend your life in lament
until your eyes bleed
this place's blind sorrow.

Coffee

No one before the discovery of coffee
ever woke up. The drowsiness
of history till that moment
appears in its very wars and murders, all conducted
with the lethargy of one
who can't get started and is mightily annoyed,
in a placid way, at having
forgotten his dream. Even the torturing
was somnolent, as though an idle attempt
to reproduce a nightmare. Even the victim
couldn't believe he was awake.

Before coffee, the only ones awake
were the gatherers
in the dense forests—shame-mans, as we call them
for some reason with a sleepy
childish wrong diction we persist in, because vanished
childhood is dear to us. Coffee
had always been there where the ancient gatherers were
and are to this day, in their contracting leafage
and perforated canopy. For them, there was never a time
"before coffee." Coffee was a phenomenon of dawn.

When we discovered it: that was the watershed of time.
Then, on the side where there had always been coffee, time
came flowing down to eternity as it always had; on the other side,
where with us there was newly coffee, time
bubbled up, rose to a spate, to excitement, to further
fervency beyond coffee itself,
if such be possible: coffee
provided the idea.

Coffee, of course, is not, in these regions of speed of ours,
a thing. It is a norm,
an unachievable ideal. No one can roast, grind,
and brew the coffee that is truly coffee,
that wakes the drinker up
to real awoken-ness. More than Guinevere
and Launcelot, it is an image
that gratifies the self-involvement of the few, almost blind
to the pathos of the inadequacy of their romantic
re-enactments, and that crushes the many
with the hopelessness of measuring up—measuring out, that is,
the proper measures
to get the perfect cup.

O coffee, my love, greatness
and pettiness of the human, aspiration
and refusal of aspiration, discovery of the beyond
in the tree and berry, discovery
of beauty in the pot and the mouth, and rejection
of the discovery in favor of
whatever we sort of can achieve,
let me steep you now, and may any
approximation I get of the thing
I dream you, however much too bitter
and over-sweetened it is,
like life, this life we lead, creakily trying
to bend down in the cold far enough
to tie our shoes, wake me
to an alertness
that dimly I imagine.

A Poem Written "in Real Time" about What I Was Doing as I Wrote It

I was eating a cookie and sipping black coffee
at my tiny desk as I read a poem
about terror, death, how even these are forgotten,
and one's own childhood—a blue lamb
hugged till its head came off, then laid in a closet
and kept with love for a few more months
until the child became other—one's childhood
becomes a straggle of glimpses, images
lying like some puddles after a big rain,
shrinking, separating, gleaming in the sun over the vast
dazzle of the land, drying away, winking
out of existence one by one. And you
are sitting in the dusty attic of your parents' home,
doing the work of winding it up, cleaning it out,
and you turn over some things, a scapular, a neckerchief clasp-ring
in cheap metal with a wolf's face engraved, a grade four essay
in fervent praise of Edgar Allan Poe, and you wonder
who you were and you can't remember
and don't know. That was the poem. The cookie,
a small rectangle of shortbread covered by a sheet
of milk chocolate with the impression of a famous chateau hotel
stamped into it, was the best cookie from the beginning of the world
to its eventual end. I don't know why I found it, why
it fell to me, me alone, in all the ages. In 1480,
the King of Portugal could not have had such a cookie,
let alone this one, for all his wealth, if he had sent
ships over all the seas, as he alone
in all the world could. Today, billions
can have this cookie. They're searching for it
in all the omnipresent packaging. It was sitting on my desk

on a small plate my grandmother gave us for our wedding,
and I ate it bit by bit so it could be the sweetness,
instead of cream and sugar, to the bitter coffee.
This was the best reading of a poem by a great, joyful
and disconsolate poet there ever had been
and ever would be. And it was mine. This is not
as naive a poem as you think it is. I don't even mind
if you say it's correct except that it happened to you, not me,
and really was not a cookie, a coffee, and a poem.
Though you would be wrong.

All I Can Say

That girl was burned alive, then shot,
as she said her prayers. Not to her murderers,
not for mercy. What then? For herself
or her father there—that some intervention
would save them? Or would save him at least?
Were they for that? For all of us? I don't know.
They were silent. Was she praying to be
comforted? To be killed in her praying,
and by that means preserved in faithfulness
to her upbringing? Were the prayers for that?
I know what the bullets after the burning were for:
she was still praying. But the prayers—
were they maybe not for anything,
only to be with someone: a god,
her childhood, the people of her good old days?
I can't say. They were silent. All I can say is
she was praying while she was burned and shot.

Pilgrims across My Work Space

My work space is very small, so in the mornings
I have to carefully fold up
the tea towel with the printed drawing of Jane Austen's
St. Nicholas at Chawton that serves
for a tablecloth, and push it to the remotest corner
of the narrow desk, and place the saucer with cookie crumbs
and the cup with coffee dregs on top of it. To do this,
I move aside my book to the floor, my notebook
to the lap drawer, my pencil to the left, and then
when breakfast is cleared off and the desk is a pure field again
of softly glowing beechwood-coloured varnish, I have to
move them all back. I used to hate this. In other words,
one world I lived in then in my heart was a boundless
landscape of lava
flowing contradictorily against itself and at the same time stuck
as if already frozen stone forever. Now, however,
God knows why, I love it all. When I bring back the pencil,
I love to study it the way I held, at three years old,
a painted lead rocket, boat, or car
with an eternal satisfaction, and loved to move them
over the carpets and through the air. This pencil is
a masterpiece of shape, of human design. Poised in my hand,
its elegance surpasses that of any starship,
and unlike a starship's, its nose is pointed down,
to the desk surface, earth surface,
never to crash but travel there far farther
than galaxies. Through its crystal (plastic) sides you can see
the clever workings of its tubes and springs. This ship
does not hold its numerous crew inside
but outside—me, admiring the pencil
caught up in my hand. And so

the landscape I have in mind now
is the land of summer, mild always if crossed
by droughts and wrecking storms at times. It advances
outward in vast meadows enclosing woods,
penetrated and explored by roads
that narrow into tracks up into hills, and then mountains,
so that in this lush summer there can be snow too,
and bare rocky ground. The people who are trekking
across it are so young that they never are
and never can be tired,
and all they know is the excitement of maybe someday
finding something, and they are so old
that they know much, know everything
people can know, and are journeying to
a renowned and ancient shrine. Impossible combination.
Just how old are these people, really? As old
as the truly human. Just where are they,
actually? On the true earth,
because without knowing it, they're grateful.
It comes naturally.

The Baptist

I can't say what I wait for
or what you should expect,
just what you have to do: come down
into the river. This goat-yellow stream
pouring from God knows where—
a cave or the sky,
the cave of the sky—
its shallow depth,
shallow drowning:
the whole of death's in it
and a coming back up to the mud-and-dust bank,
clumps of lean trees
badly screening off the wilderness,
murmur of the terrified, the lonely,
gawkers, pious madwomen...Maybe someone among them,
already with us, knows the stream
with its unmirrored sky, its weary long edges,
as footing and vista of the sun in the blood.

After Tagore

In the dull rainy morning, you walk
silent as the night. No one sees you.
Day keeps its eyes closed to the wet wind.
Cold fog is like an old grey sheet
pulled up to shut out the dawn.
You are the only walker in the empty street,
O my friend. O my belovèd. My door
is open. Don't pass me by like a dream.

A Room Inside and Out

What is to be is not revealed.
But what you have said with me
and what you have done with me
make a melody, the memory
of the words and acts
continuing in me, unfolding,
meeting, marrying,
leaving, going on together,
together like us and apart. I lie
in my bed and they're with me
silent in my ear. They come
into me and they are me,
they meet me there and I turn,
greet them, and we go on,
it grows dark, I'm alone with
them within me, and I sleep then
or I almost sleep, I move toward sleep
and I have no need to see.

Elsewhere

It's raining. No one's coming.
I have a porch to sit on.
Water on leaves.
The soft ending-rain dripping
onto flower beds
from the eaves. Chill quiet.
A streak of mauve and orange
in the west behind the still
green trees now ceasing
to shine, turning
an ashen black I love.
The end of dusk.
Nothing. No one.
I'll stay here.
I'll never go back.
Everything will be fine.

NOTES

Beyond

"It's an ill wind that blows no good" is of course a very old commonplace but here it is meant as the first line of the song "Share Your Love with Me" (Don Robey, Al Braggs) being sung on the jukebox in the bar by Bobby "Blue" Bland.

A Muse

Terpsichore is usually the muse of lyric poetry and the dance, but in other versions, of lyric poetry and flute playing. The name is pronounced turp-SIK-or-ee.

The Little Known

After Kakinomoto Hitomaro, "Praise of the Empress Jitō"

A Woman in a Painting but Not So

Compare Corot's *Flesselles, une Rue avec une Paysanne et sa Vache* (*Flesselles, a Road with a Peasant Woman and Her Cow*), ca. 1862–65. The poem resembles this painting but is a composite of various Corot paintings and the scene is primarily an invented one. That is, the poem describes a Corot painting of a scene and person that Corot did not have the opportunity to paint but that, more essentially, he did paint in all his painting of this type: enigmatic still repose, where the persons possess a peace and a grasp of existence that they do not, in the usual sense, possess. So the particular woman in the painting in the poem is in a painting of Corot's but is not.

Published in *The High Window* (UK). Thanks to David Cooke, poet and editor of The High Window Press.

Credal Statement

Published in *The High Window*

To Those Who Like to Say “I’m Not Much for Poetry”
Published in *The High Window*

Dead Skunk in the Road
Published in *Verse Afire*. Thanks to poet Bunny Iskov, editor of the magazine, for ideas about relineating the poem from its original version.

A Flower Giving Names to Eve and Adam
Published in *The High Window*

Where
Published in *FreeFall*. Thanks to poet and editor Micheline Maylor.

Why Do We Read?
The translation in italics—really a free imitation—of poetry by Enheduanna is based on the prose translations in the Electronic Text Corpus of Sumerian Literature (ETCSL) https://etcsl.orinst.ox.ac.uk/. My version is a portion of Enheduanna’s “Temple Hymn 7,” one of three (out of the forty-two temple hymns attributed to her in antiquity) that today are held most likely to have been in fact written by the poet and priestess, who lived around 2300 BCE. The specific translation texts I used (accessed online throughout 2021–22) are sections 87–95 and 95–99; the specific locale of these translations is https://etcsl.orinst.ox.ac.uk/cgi-bin/etcsl.cgi?text=t.4.80.1#. I also used some additional material from neighbouring sections of the website and other sources of knowledge about Sumeria.

Enheduanna, the first author in history to be known by name, was a daughter of Sargon the Great, who is thought of as the first empire-builder. She was high priestess of Inanna. After Sargon’s death, there was (apparently—the reconstruction is made in part from poems attributed to Enheduanna) a revolt against the Sargon dynasty in the city of Ur by Ur’s king, Lugal-Ane. Enheduanna was required to support the new regime, but refused, and was driven out of her temple and city. This is largely the subject of *Nin me šara*, “Lady of Innumerable Powers”—a different poem from the one I translated.

There are many allusions in "Why Do We Read?" It seems useful to identify the ones that occur in the last eight stanzas of the first part of the poem and that aren't more or less identified in the text.

The poem of mine referred to in the phrase "and by me a little earlier" is "Don Juan" (*The Tradition,* 1986). The Montale poem is "L'anguilla" / "The Eel" (*La bufera e altro,* 1956). The Jiménez poem is "Cielo" / "Heaven," or "Sky" (*Diario de un poeta reciéncasado,* 1916). The phrase "the wilds, where lions roam" is drawn from and refers to Blake, *The Marriage of Heaven and Hell,* "The Argument." The phrase "to lie down and be a pebble by the road" is paraphrased from and refers to Octavio Paz's "Dama huasteca" / "Huastec Lady" from *¿Aguila o sol?* (1950). The poem concludes, "al lado del camino; de noche, un río que fluye al costado del hombre." / "I will say her secret: by day, she is a stone by the side of the road; by night, a river that flows to the side [the coast; the ribs] of man."

Vagueness

Published in *FreeFall*

An Angel

Published in *FreeFall*

Word and Silence: After Neruda

This poem is made by translating, paraphrasing, collaging, and adding to lines and passages from three Neruda poems from *Plenos poderes* (1962); the title is translated by Alastair Reid as "fully empowered." First stanza: after scattered lines from "La palabra." Second stanza: after "Serenata." Third stanza: after the last stanza of "En la torre."

The Gift

Published in *Devour.* Thanks to poet and publisher Tai Grove and poet and editor Bruce Kauffman.

Letter to Breton

The subtitle of this poem, *Breton à l'avant de soi / Breton out ahead of us*, is the title of a book (2001) by Bonnefoy.

On a Thought of Juan Ramón Jiménez

The thought is the first half of poem 31, section III, of *La realidad invisible*, never published though often referred to by Jiménez in his lifetime (1881–1958) and the source of many poems that he had placed in various self-selected anthologies of his work. The book was discovered in archives by Antonio Sánchez Romeralo in 1970 and published in 1983.

And what difference does all of it make
if as fire we can consume
each pain and sorrow—O passion—in a star;
if we can make
out of the immense black night
our immense illuminated joy?

In the Motet of Mondonville

Jean-Joseph Cassanéa de Mondonville (1711–72). *Grand Motet: Dominus regnavit* (Psalm 92)

Gloria: the song by The Cadillacs, which became a "doo wop" anthem, with versions by dozens of groups

Hearing from You

Published in *Ampersand Review*; thank you to the editor-in-chief, poet Paul Vermeersch, and all the staff.

Quibble with Hegel

My quibble is with Hegel's famous metaphor of the oak tree and acorn (*Phenomenology of Spirit*, "Preface," para. 12). "When we wish to see an oak with its powerful trunk, its spreading branches, and its mass of foliage, we are not satisfied if instead we are shown an acorn. In the same way, science, the crowning glory of a spiritual world, is not completed in its initial stages." Well, we're not satisfied with anything, but in so far as we can approach satisfaction, it ought to be with each "stage" of a thing, especially a person, because each stage, while it is indeed an acorn, is also complete and unsurpassable in itself. In this regard I think primarily of the child. Anyone who has had to do at all closely and sympathetically with a child knows that the child is not an insufficient adult or "merely" a being developing toward adulthood, although the child is that also—in addition to what it is presently. Or rather, its developing toward something else is (only) a part and form of what it is now.

In his preceding paragraph, Hegel had used the metaphor of the child, the prenatal child coming to birth and being born, as a metaphor for enlightenment, or rather, for mental/spiritual progress: "...just as with a child, who after a long silent period of nourishment draws his first breath and shatters the gradualness of only quantitative growth—it makes a qualitative leap and is born—so too, in bringing itself to cultural maturity, spirit ripens slowly and quietly into its new shape, dissolving bit by bit the structure of its previous world..." until the process "is interrupted by the break of day, which in a flash and at a single stroke brings to view the structure of the new world." (para. 11)

This reminds one of the Spanish idiom for parturition: *dar a la luz*, give to the light. Jiménez uses that expression in addressing the same thing in far more comprehensive, exact, and correct terms than Hegel's:

> Things give birth. I
> love them, and they, with me,
> through a rainbow of grace
> give me children, give me children!

While we are incapable of not hoping for an overall, definitive "progress" and achievement, a fact that is more or less the point of Hegel's remarks, it is more true that anything worthy of the term progress in the honorific sense we give that word happens or can happen in every moment of every person—and always could and did so, back to "the caveman." There is not one moment, whether in a person's history or in the history of humanity, that can be diminished or demeaned as merely preliminary and inferior.

The process of wedding between self and the given world happens constantly and turns each moment on earth into a rainbow that is simultaneously the active opening of the womb, through which come children. In Jiménez the grateful awe of this occurrence is the pure emotion found in the doubling of the outcry of recognition. In intellectual discussion, attention is often mentioned and properly given an essential role. But if the discussion of attention, and if attention itself, has not noticed the permanent and total presence of human creativity—life, hope—in every human moment, then attention has not really been paid.

A still more important dimension of the error here is that this sort of thinking originates and is constantly expressed in the ladder of consciousness idea that is omnipresent: experience, art, science, or interpretation, in order of supposed altitude. In fact, poetry is positioned between, comprehends both the others, and tries to unite interpretation and experience, refusing to let the former fly free in its arrogance. Poetry is the superior form of consciousness. Science, interpretation, are best thought of as a sort of translation of poetry, and (at one further remove) of experience, into intellectual-rational terms so that some of the content can be had by scientific humanity, which has lost the ability to read the original language. Of course, such a translation depends on the interpreter or scientist himself/herself being able to read the original, and this is a rare occurrence.

Hegel translations: *The Phenomenology of Spirit,* tr. Terry Pinkard (2018), p. 9

When I Was a Child

The title phrase, which appears elsewhere in *Great Silent Ballad* including as the title of another poem, is a translation of Hölderlin's phrase, "Da ich ein Knabe war," which is the title and first line of one of his short odes. I also mean to refer to Peter Handke's "Lied vom Kindsein" / "Song of Childhood." Its first line, "Als das Kind Kind war," "When the child was a child," is recalling Hölderlin, including in the purposeful change from "boy" to "child."

When Chappie Got Out

Published in *Verse Afire*

I Know I Was

"the sky is crying": the song by Elmore James

Seeds People Thoughts

The last four lines are a translation-adaptation of an image of Juan Ramón Jiménez's from *Diario de un poeta reciencasado / Diary of a Newlywed Poet* (1916), poem XIV, "Tarde en ninguna parte (Mar de adentro)" / "Evening Nowhere (Inner Sea)": "¡Este instante infinito—cielo bajo—, / entre una larga y lenta / ola del corazón—despierta sangre— / y una antigua, olvidada / y nuevamente vista estrella!" / "This infinite instant—the low sky— / between a long, slow / sea swell of the heart—awakened blood— / and an ancient, forgotten / and newly noticed star."

About twenty years later, Czesław Miłosz arrived at the same idea, in flower imagery: "Oh, if there were in me one seed without rust, / ... / I would wait quietly... / till a wildflower, a stone in the field stare up / with the disc of an unknown new face." ("The Song," dated "Wilno 1934").

Published in *Ars Notoria* (UK). Thanks to poetry editor Sudeep Sen.

You Don't Know

Published in *The Walrus*. Thanks to the editor-in-chief, poet Carmine Starnino.

House

Maybe the word "rind" at the end here doesn't un-disquiet or dis-disquiet but in fact disquiets? I'll just say that "rind" is a minor keyword in the book, occurring twice in "Dancer Speaking," from which the book title comes, and once in "On a Thought of Juan Ramón Jiménez."

Published by *Vallum* in the print magazine and as an online video; thanks to publisher and editor Eleni Zisimatos and all the staff.

The Crossing

Published in *Ars Notoria*

Pawnshop Row

Published in *Ars Notoria*

This Is You

Published in *Ars Notoria*

The Nature of Thought

The italicized opening lines are quoted from my poem "My Method," *Here* (Contraband Press: Portland, Maine; 1975). Thanks to poet and editor Bruce Holsapple. Published in *Ars Notoria*

A Blue Bicycle

Cp. Czesław Miłosz, "Yellow Bicycle", *Selected and Last Poems 1931-2004* (2006), p. 187. Published in *Ars Notoria*

Householder

"I dwell in Possibility": Dickinson, poem 466, Franklin ed., 1988

Liking to Be a Tree

"Stubborn task": *lavorare stanca*, "stubborn work", title of a book of poems by Pavese

After Tagore

Gitanjali, poem 22

. . .

Acknowledgements

My profound thanks to all at Anansi, especially to Poetry editor Kevin Connolly, to Michael Redhill, who acted as substantive editor of *Great Silent Ballad* and made suggestions crucial to its final form, and to Peter Norman for alert and helpful copyediting. Thanks also to designers Greg Tabor and Lucia Kim, production editor Jenny McWha, and assistant editor Leslie Joy Ahenda.

Author photograph by Steve Payne

A. F. MORITZ's entire post-education life has been spent in Toronto; he was the city's poet laureate 2019–23. He has written twenty-two books of poetry. His works with Anansi, since 2004, have received the Griffin Poetry Prize, the ReLit Award, the Bess Hokin Prize, and the Raymond Souster Award, and were finalists for the Governor General's Award (twice) and the Trillium Award. He has received a Guggenheim Fellowship, the Ingram Merrill Fellowship, and the Award in Literature of the American Academy of Arts and Letters.